D1601433

A CHRONOLOGY OF U.S. SPECIAL OPS

by **Michael Burgan**

Consultant:
Raymond L. Puffer, PhD
Historian, Retired
Edwards Air Force Base History Office

CAPSTONE PRESS
a capstone imprint

Connect is published by Capstone Press,
1710 Roe Crest Drive, North Mankato, Minnesota 56003
www.mycapstone.com

Library of Congress Cataloging-in-Publication Data
Names: Burgan, Michael.
Title: A Chronology of U.S. special ops / by Michael Burgan.
Description: North Mankato, Minnesota: Capstone Press, [2017] | Series:
   Connect. U.S. special ops | Includes bibliographical references and index.
   | Audience: Ages 8-14
Identifiers: LCCN 2015042280
   ISBN 9781515718505 (library binding)
   ISBN 9781515718536 (eBook PDF)
Subjects: LCSH: Special forces (Military science)—Juvenile literature.
   Special operations (Military science)—United States—History—Juvenile
literature.
Classification: LCC UA34.S64 B85 2017 | DDC 356/.160973—dc23
LC record available at http://lccn.loc.gov/2015042280

Editorial Credits
Brenda Haugen, editor; Steve Mead, designer;
Jo Miller, media researcher; Katy LaVigne, production specialist

Image Credits
Alamy: Everett Collection Historical, 23, Mary Evans Picture Library, 9;
AP Images, 32; Corbis, 7, , 13, Bettmann, 24, 27, 29, Xinhua Press/yslb pak,
42; Getty Images: AFP/Alexander Joe, 38, Archive Photos/Ed Vebell, 8,
Archive Photos/Underwood Archives, 16, The LIFE Picture Collection/
Bernard Hoffman, 19, The LIFE Picture Collection/Larry Burrows, 30, The
LIFE Picture Collection/US Army/Sgt. Michael Bogdanowicz, 34; Newscom:
Everett Collection, 14, ZUMA Press/M Martin Cuaron, 4; U.S. Navy SEAL
and SWCC photo, Cover; Wikimedia, 11, courtesy United States Special
Operations Command, 40, NARA, 21, Sgt. Kimberly Yearyean, 36, Staff Sgt.
Robert Storm, 44; Wikipedia, 37

Design Elements
Shutterstock: Alexander Smulskiy, Artur. B, Axi, Dn Br, Gallinago_media,
Nik Merkulov, Svetlana Avv, vadimmmus, Yulia Glam

Printed and bound in Canada.
009649F16

TABLE OF CONTENTS

CHAPTER 1

BEFORE MODERN WARFARE

In the mountains of Afghanistan, a U.S. Special Operations team enters a small village by helicopter. Afghan troops help in this nighttime raid to capture a **terrorist** leader. A previous raid gave the Americans **intelligence** on where the terrorist is hiding. Quickly and quietly, the soldiers find his house. Then, guns drawn, the Americans and Afghans knock down the door and capture their target. They never fire a shot.

Special Operations forces like these in Afghanistan are a key part of today's warfare. All branches of the U.S. military use these highly trained forces. They can gather intelligence, rescue **hostages**, and fight deep behind enemy lines.

terrorist—someone who uses violence and threats to frighten people

intelligence—secret information about an enemy's plans or action

hostage—a person held against his or her will

4

Today's Special Operations forces use some of the world's best weapons and high-tech gear to carry out their work. But that was not the case for the first special operations members who carried out similar secret and dangerous missions. Even before the United States was a country, some Americans risked their lives fighting enemy forces in small groups. During the 20th century, military leaders expanded Special Operations forces and the roles they play.

U.S. Special Operations soldiers watched two Black Hawk helicopters prepare to land in Afghanistan in 2012.

THE FIRST RANGERS

One special ops force still in use today is the Army Rangers. The first American Rangers fought during colonial days. In 1754 Great Britain and France went to war over who would control lands west of the 13 American colonies. The British recruited Americans to help them fight the French and their Indian **allies**.

Major Robert Rogers led several hundred soldiers called Rogers' Rangers. Most came from New Hampshire. They knew the local lands better than the British did and had experience fighting American Indians on the frontier. Rogers and his men scouted enemy positions and carried out raids. They also captured French soldiers and gathered intelligence from them. During the winter the Rangers trudged through the forest on snowshoes. At times they traveled hundreds of miles into lands controlled by the French.

Rogers' Rangers used snowshoes to cross snowy terrain on a march during the French and Indian War.

ally—a person or country united with another for a common purpose

FACT

Major Robert Rogers wrote down a list of 28 rules he expected his men to follow. These included what kinds of weapons to carry and how to march properly. Along with using a musket, the Rangers sometimes fought hand-to-hand using small axes and swords.

FIGHTING FOR INDEPENDENCE

The British won the French and Indian War. In the following years, more and more Americans wanted independence from Great Britain. The American Revolution began in 1775, and Rangers fought again. Daniel Morgan of Virginia led the Corps of Rangers. His Rangers were expert shooters. They helped the Americans win the Battle of Saratoga in 1777.

Daniel Morgan led his troops in battle in Virginia.

In 1780 and 1781, Francis Marion led other Rangers on raids against British troops in South Carolina. He and his men often moved through swampy lands, and Marion earned the nickname the Swamp Fox.

SECRECY AT SEA

During the American Revolution, David Bushnell helped plan a secret mission that would be similar to future Navy Special Operations. Bushnell built the world's first combat submarine, the *Turtle*. To move, the *Turtle* used small propellers turned by its pilot's hands and feet. In the summer of 1776, Bushnell taught Ezra Lee how to use the *Turtle*. Lee tried to attach a mine under a British ship using the *Turtle*. He failed to attach the mine, but he escaped before British sailors could catch him. More than 150 years later, Navy divers also secretly planted explosives on enemy ships.

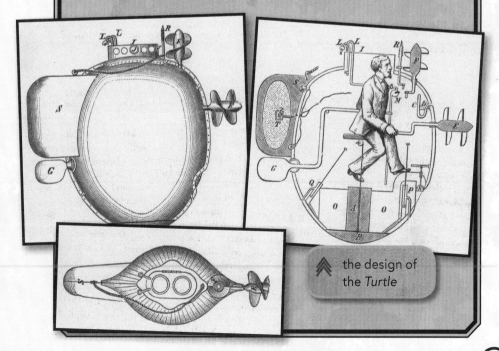

the design of the *Turtle*

SPECIAL OPERATIONS OF THE CIVIL WAR

In 1861 Americans found themselves at war with each other, as northern and southern states fought the Civil War (1861–1865). In 1862 southern lawmakers called for the creation of Ranger units. The most famous of these Rangers was John Mosby of Virginia. He led raids and scouting missions that provided important information on northern troops.

★★★★★
FACT

Mosby and his men rode off separately after their missions. This made it hard for northern troops to capture them. Mosby was called the Gray Ghost for the way he disappeared after his raids.

Confederate Cavalry Colonel John Mosby (second row, fourth from left) and some of his men

Mosby received permission to form his own group of Rangers in 1863. They were free to do as they pleased without reporting to southern officials. In one daring raid, Mosby and several dozen of his men went into a Union camp and kidnapped an enemy general. On other missions Mosby's Rangers captured northern horses and soldiers and at times also fought small battles. In one battle in 1863, the Rangers captured or killed 40 northern troops without losing any men of their own.

★★☆☆

CHAPTER 2

THE WORLD AT WAR

The United States did not have major Special Operations forces again until World War II (1939–1945). The country's main enemies during World War II were Germany, Japan, and Italy. American troops fought in many places around the world, and starting in 1942, the Office of Strategic Services (OSS) helped them. While the OSS wasn't officially a Special Operations force, it carried out many of the same types of missions future special ops would. Many OSS members knew foreign languages and served as spies. Their training included learning how to parachute into enemy lands and fight in hand-to-hand combat. They also taught foreign allies these same skills. After the war many OSS members joined the Central Intelligence Agency (CIA). Created in 1947, the CIA continues to be the country's major spy agency.

★★★★★
FACT

OSS agents sometimes carried special weapons, such as a pen that was actually a gun or an explosive that looked like a lump of coal. Some also wore shoes with hollow bottoms so they could carry secret messages.

commando—specially trained soldier who can carry out surprise attacks, often in small groups

Small groups of OSS **commandos** carried out many important missions in Europe. Some blew up railways the Germans used to move supplies. Others gathered information on where the Germans placed mines and large guns. Others staged small attacks to trick the Germans into thinking larger battles were about to take place. These attacks forced the Germans to move their troops away from the spots the Allies actually planned to strike.

News was posted outside a military camp in Burma during World War II.

THE JEDBURGHS

Some OSS agents joined Jedburgh teams. A Jedburgh team usually had one member each from Great Britain, France, and the United States. The teams parachuted behind German lines to work with the local **resistance** fighters. The Jedburghs carried poison pills they were supposed to swallow if they got caught. They were prepared to die rather than risk being tortured and give the Germans useful information.

a Jedburgh team by a B-24 from which they would parachute into German-occupied France

resistance—the people of an invaded nation who work together to drive out the invaders, often in secret

ambush—a surprise attack

The Jedburghs sometimes directly battled German troops. In 1944 several Jedburgh teams and French fighters **ambushed** advancing German troops. Using their machine guns and other weapons, the Allies killed more than 100 Germans.

WOMEN OF THE OSS

OSS agents working in France sometimes recruited local women to work for them. One was known only by the codename Maria. She spoke German, so the OSS trained her as a spy. She parachuted into Germany and pretended to be a nurse. The OSS gave her fake ID papers that said she was a German citizen. Traveling through the country, Maria gathered information about the location of German troops. She took this information back to the OSS agents in France.

THE DEADLY SKILLS OF THE OSS

Some OSS members were part of Operational Groups. Larger than Jedburgh teams, these groups also fought behind German lines. This chart shows some of their achievements:

 KNOWN GERMANS KILLED: 461

 KNOWN GERMANS WOUNDED: 467

 KNOWN GERMAN PRISONERS: 10,021

 AIRCRAFT SHOT DOWN: 3

 VEHICLES DESTROYED: 33

 ROADS MINED: 17

 BRIDGES DESTROYED: 32

SPECIAL OPERATIONS AT SEA

The U.S. Navy developed its first special operations forces during World War II. In 1942 the Navy began training sailors to perform dangerous missions close to enemy shores. The training continued the next year as the Navy formed Naval Combat Demolition Units (NCDUs) and Underwater Demolition Teams (UDTs).

Both teams had similar missions. They carried out **reconnaissance**, looking for reefs or **obstacles** on beaches that could damage approaching Navy boats. At times they blew up the obstacles. The sailors often rowed rubber boats close to shore and then swam toward the beach.

A Navy UDT clears mines in Korea in 1950.

UDT members often swam in just bathing suits, with masks on their faces and fins on their feet. They carried only knives to defend themselves, and enemy gunners sometimes fired at them while they worked. Occasionally U.S. ships returned the fire, and the swimmers heard the **shells** whistling overhead. UDT training and methods would later be used by Navy SEALs.

★★★★★
FACT

British military divers were first called frogmen because they wore green suits while underwater. After World War II, the name was also used for UDT divers.

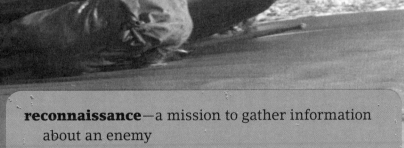

reconnaissance—a mission to gather information about an enemy

obstacle—something that gets in the way or prevents someone from doing something

shell—a metal container filled with gunpowder and fired from a large gun

THE RETURN OF THE RANGERS

As in past wars, soldiers called Rangers also took part in World War II. The most famous belonged to an Army unit called Merrill's Marauders. They were named for their commander, Frank Merrill. Formed in 1943, the next year they operated behind Japanese lines in Burma, which is now called Myanmar. They often surprised the enemy and were able to defeat much larger forces. Merrill's Marauders traveled more than 1,000 miles (1,609 kilometers) on foot through jungles to cut Japan's supply lines and prevent its soldiers from communicating with one another. The Marauders also captured an airfield that was under Japanese control. Today's Army Rangers trace their direct roots to Merrill's force, while still realizing the importance of earlier Ranger units.

During World War II, the Army had its own air force. Some of the Army planes helped with special operations missions in Europe. They dropped supplies to OSS agents and commandos fighting behind enemy lines. In Asia Army pilots called Air Commandos brought in troops and supplies to help the British fight the Japanese. Future special operations crews of the U.S. Air Force would carry out similar missions.

Merrill's Marauders hike through a jungle in Burma in 1944 in an effort to help defeat the Japanese.

SPECIAL OPERATIONS TEAMWORK

Members of various Special Operations units worked together on D-Day, the day the Allies invaded Normandy, France. This invasion began on June 6, 1944, but before that, OSS agents had already parachuted into France. They gathered intelligence and worked with the local resistance. Jedburgh teams also went behind enemy lines. Some parachuted out of Army planes that were painted black. The color made the planes hard to spot at night.

When the actual D-Day battle came, Naval Combat Demolition Units worked along the beaches of Normandy. They blew up steel and concrete barriers the Germans had set up as obstacles. Once the barriers were gone, Allied soldiers and tanks raced ashore.

Some of the soldiers included Army Rangers. One general shouted, "Rangers, lead the way!" That is now the motto of today's Rangers. Members of one Ranger unit used ropes to climb up a high, rocky cliff and destroy huge artillery pieces that threatened the beach below. The work of Special Operations forces before, during, and after D-Day helped the Allies win World War II.

Allied forces make their way into France after the D-Day battle.

★★★☆

CREATING TODAY'S SPECIAL OPERATIONS FORCES

After World War II, the United States changed its military in several ways. The government shut down the OSS in 1945. Two years later it created a new spy organization, the Central Intelligence Agency (CIA). Some agents still received military training. In 1947 the government also ended the Army Air Forces and created the U.S. Air Force.

FACT

The Rangers in Korea included one **company** of soldiers who were African-American. Two members, Warren Allen and James Queen, are in the Ranger Hall of Fame for their bravery during the war.

American soldiers sometimes fought from trenches in Korea in 1950.

Three years later Americans were fighting again, this time in Korea during the Korean War (1950– 1953). For the first time Army Rangers used parachutes to drop behind enemy lines.

In 1952 the Army created the Special Forces. Members operated somewhat like Jedburgh teams but with 12 men instead of three. The Army Special Forces gathered intelligence, worked with local allies, and carried out **sabotage**. Members did not actually fight in Korea.

But Navy UDTs did fight in the Korean War. For the first time, they came ashore to blow up targets, such as tunnels and bridges.

company—a U.S. military group made up of three to five platoons of soldiers

sabotage—damage or destruction of property that is done on purpose

THE VIETNAM WAR

Starting in the late 1950s, the United States fought in the Vietnam War in Vietnam and neighboring Asian countries. In 1961 President John F. Kennedy saw the value of using the Army Special Forces to fight a new kind of war. Kennedy thought the military would more often fight small groups of enemy forces rather than a large army. The Army Special Forces were trained for that kind of fighting, and they served across Vietnam.

FACT

Army Rangers wore black berets and then tan ones. Members of the different Army Air Commando units also have their own colored berets.

THE GREEN BERETS

Members of the Army Special Forces sometimes wore green caps, called berets. The caps were not part of their official uniform, and Army officials did not like them. But President John F. Kennedy did. Before he came to meet Special Forces troops, he told their commander to have them wear the green berets. He thought the caps made the troops stand out from other soldiers. He said the caps should be part of the Army Special Forces' uniform, and after that the men were known as the Green Berets.

Army Special Forces soldiers show South Vietnamese men how to use weapons to defend their villages against enemy attacks.

SEALS IN ACTION

In 1961 the Navy also prepared for the new kind of warfare Kennedy imagined. To meet the new needs, the Navy created the SEALs. The SEALs took over some of the duties of the UDTs. The SEALs' name stood for how they might enter combat—by sea, air, and land. Today the SEALs go through the longest and perhaps hardest training of any of the U.S. Special Operations forces.

After the first SEALs completed their training, some went to Vietnam in 1962 to help train America's allies in South Vietnam. Most of the first SEALs later saw intense action fighting in the Vietnam War.

The SEALs worked in small groups. They gathered intelligence from local residents before staging attacks. Navy boats brought them up rivers. Then the SEALs often sailed smaller wooden boats called sampans to their targets. Some SEALs also traveled to missions by helicopter. On their various missions, they destroy weapons and supplies, rescue prisoners, and much more.

FACT

SEALs worked with all kinds of weapons. The first SEALs trained with bows and arrows so they could silently kill enemies. Other SEALs practiced transporting and setting up small **nuclear** bombs. One bomb could wipe out a large battlefield or a small city. The SEALS, though, never had to use these deadly weapons.

nuclear—having to do with the energy created by splitting atoms; nuclear bombs use this energy to cause an explosion

Navy SEALs used camouflage to stay hidden in the jungles of Vietnam.

A DANGEROUS MISSION

Like the SEALs, the Green Berets went from training South Vietnamese troops to fighting actual battles. They carried out raids on enemy bases along with conducting reconnaissance. One of their most daring missions came in 1970. The Green Berets were chosen to rescue dozens of U.S. prisoners of war being held at Son Tay prison camp in North Vietnam.

The Army Special Forces trained for months. They built a copy of the prison in Florida and carried out 170 practice raids. In November 56 Green Berets flew in helicopters to the real prison camp. Some of the men landed near the prison camp so they could blow up the walls. Another group landed inside the prison to round up the American prisoners. Meanwhile a third group battled enemy soldiers based just outside the prison.

The whole mission took just under 30 minutes, and no Green Berets were killed. There was just one problem: The Americans were no longer at Son Tay. The North Vietnamese had moved them before the raid, and the Americans were never rescued. But the mission was used to teach future Special Operations forces how to carry out difficult raids.

FACT

The prisoners once held in Son Tay were finally released in 1973. They met some of the Green Berets who had tried to rescue them and told the soldiers that the effort to rescue them had boosted their spirits. The prisoners knew they had not been forgotten.

General Leroy Manor planned the raid on the Son Tay prison camp.

Army Special Forces Captain Vernon Gillespie (center) leads soldiers through a jungle stream in Vietnam.

A LOST WAR

Air Commandos also took part in the Son Tay raid. They flew the helicopters as well as some planes that took part in the mission. Throughout the war the Air Commandos carried out reconnaissance too.

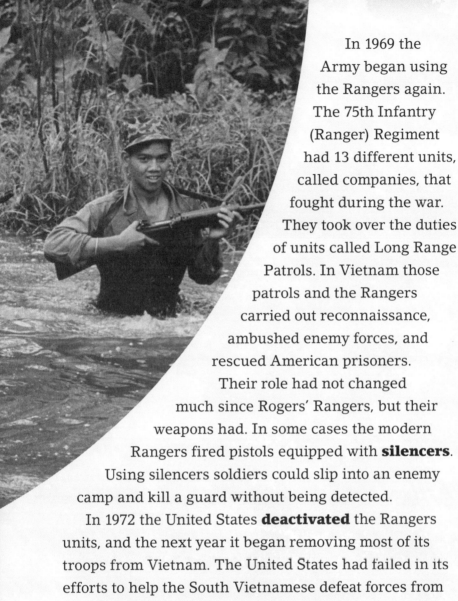

In 1969 the Army began using the Rangers again. The 75th Infantry (Ranger) Regiment had 13 different units, called companies, that fought during the war. They took over the duties of units called Long Range Patrols. In Vietnam those patrols and the Rangers carried out reconnaissance, ambushed enemy forces, and rescued American prisoners. Their role had not changed much since Rogers' Rangers, but their weapons had. In some cases the modern Rangers fired pistols equipped with **silencers**. Using silencers soldiers could slip into an enemy camp and kill a guard without being detected.

In 1972 the United States **deactivated** the Rangers units, and the next year it began removing most of its troops from Vietnam. The United States had failed in its efforts to help the South Vietnamese defeat forces from the north. While Ranger companies were deactivated, the Army Special Forces and Air Force Special Operations were cut back.

silencer—an attachment for a gun that reduces noise when the gun is fired

deactivate—to take out of military duty

A NEW SPECIAL OPERATIONS FORCE

The U.S. military, however, knew the continuing importance of special operations. In 1980 the government used members of different forces to try to rescue 52 Americans who were being held hostage in Iran. It was a complicated mission, and it failed.

Later that year the government created the Joint Special Operations Command (JSOC) to carry out difficult missions in the future. The JSOC is now made up of the Army's Delta Force, Navy SEALs, Air Force Special Operations, and a military intelligence unit. Other special ops forces might also take part in JSOC missions. Its main goal is to fight terrorist threats against the United States. JSOC now comes under the command of the larger U.S. Special Operations Command.

A burned-out U.S. helicopter sits in front of an abandoned chopper in Iran. The aircraft were part of a failed mission to rescue hostages in 1980.

THE "SECRET ARMY" OF JSOC

The JSOC relies on highly skilled personnel and special equipment to carry out its mission. The equipment includes high-tech tools for gathering intelligence, such as satellites and drones. JSOC has computer experts who can shut down terrorist websites. Its military forces include the Army's Delta Force, which was founded in 1977, and SEAL Team Six. If a member is killed in combat, the government never admits it. U.S. leaders usually say the fighter died accidentally. In the field nothing on the members' uniforms reveals their name or rank. Members of the JSOC have operated in many countries around the world, including ones friendly with the United States.

★ ★ ★ ★

CHAPTER 4

THE MISSIONS CONTINUE

Since the 1980s members of the different Special Operations forces have often led U.S. troops into battle. In 1983 the United States invaded the island of Grenada. In part, the military wanted to rescue U.S. students in danger there. Rangers, Delta Force, and the Army's Special Operations **Airwing** attacked various spots on the island. Navy SEALs also took part. The forces did not have good intelligence, and they suffered some **casualties**. But they were able to rescue the Americans and take control of the island. Six years later Special Operations forces worked together again during an invasion of Panama.

U.S. Army Rangers, their faces camouflaged, gathered to discuss strategy.

airwing—a group of military aircraft

casualty—someone who is killed, wounded, or missing in a battle or in a war

Panama's leader was Manuel Noriega. He was accused of drug trafficking and other crimes. Navy SEALs and Air Force Special Operations members took over an airfield so Noriega could not escape by plane. Rangers, Green Berets, Delta Force members, and Air Force Commandos invaded other parts of the country.

Noriega fled, but Special Operations forces learned where he was hiding. They arranged for his release and brought him to the United States to stand trial for his crimes.

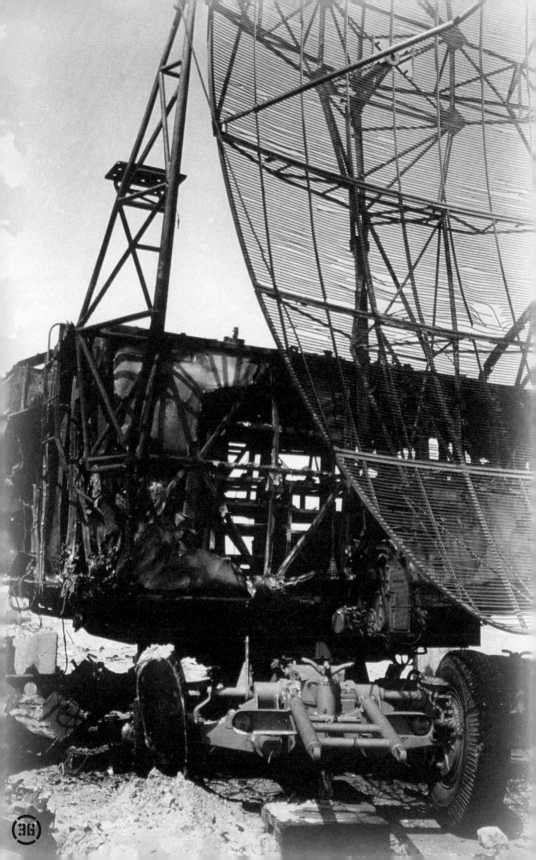

FIGHTING AROUND THE WORLD

As in the past, U.S. Special Operations units fight in many corners of the world. In 1991 some took part in the Gulf War. The United States and its allies wanted to free Kuwait, which had been invaded by neighboring Iraq. Air Force Special Operations helicopters led the assault on Iraqi radar stations before a massive air attack began. Fighting on the ground soon followed.

★★★★★
FACT

During the Gulf War, an Air Commandos helicopter crew carried out a daring daytime mission. They rescued a downed U.S. Navy pilot deep behind enemy lines. For their bravery the crew members won the Mackay Trophy. The trophy honors the most important Air Force flight of each year.

« The debris from a destroyed Iraqi radar sits in the desert after a U.S. air attack during the Gulf War.

In 1993 U.S. troops went to Somalia to keep peace between rival groups seeking power in the African country. In October Army Rangers were sent to capture two men. They did, but Somalis shot down several helicopters and killed six Rangers.

During the 1990s Special Operations forces took part in missions in countries that were once part of Yugoslavia. At times they brought food and supplies to **civilians**.

 U.S. Army Rangers wait at the Mogadishu, Somalia, airport in August 1993.

civilian—a person who is not in the military

While the Rangers and other Special Operations forces are always ready to travel around the world, some missions never happen. The United States threatened to send special operations forces to Haiti to help the elected president there in 1994. He had been forced out of office by the Haitian military. Rangers prepared to begin an assault by air, but the U.S. government made a last-minute deal that returned the Haitian president to power without an attack.

A NEW ENEMY

On September 11, 2001, Arab groups from a terrorist organization called al-Qaeda hijacked two passenger planes and crashed them into the Twin Towers of New York's World Trade Center. Other al-Qaeda members hijacked a plane and crashed it into the Pentagon, the major U.S. military building just outside Washington, D.C. Another plane hijacked by al-Qaeda crashed in Pennsylvania. All together, the attacks killed almost 3,000 people. After 9/11, fighting terrorism became a major mission for U.S. Special Operations.

A Special Operations captain uses a portable laser designator in Afghanistan in 2001 to direct Air Force and Navy bombs.

Al-Qaeda was based in Afghanistan. President George W. Bush sent Special Operations forces there to find Osama bin Laden, the leader of al-Qaeda. U.S. government leaders also wanted to replace the Taliban, Afghanistan's rulers, with a government that opposed terrorism.

The Special Operations units worked with local allies, forces from other countries, and the CIA to remove the Taliban from power. But fighting in the mountains, they were not able to capture bin Laden.

In 2003 Special Operations forces returned to Iraq to help in what became known as the Iraq War. President Bush believed Iraq's leader, Saddam Hussein, had helped terrorists and might do so again. Bush also feared that Hussein had powerful weapons of mass destruction that could kill thousands of people at once. Special Operations forces seized Iraqi airfields, dams, and oil-pumping stations. They also worked as part of a team to capture Hussein.

FACT

The U.S. Marines created its own Special Operations unit in 2006. The Marine Corps Forces Special Operations Command (MARSOC) works with other Special Operations forces to fight terrorism around the world. Today the unit is called the Raiders, to honor specially trained Marines who fought under that name during World War II.

CAPTURING BIN LADEN

U.S. combat troops remained in Iraq until 2011. They battled Iraqis who opposed the U.S. presence there. Meanwhile, fighting continued in Afghanistan, and Osama bin Laden remained on the loose. Finally, early in 2011, the United States received intelligence on the location of bin Laden's hideout in Pakistan. That May, SEAL Team Six carried out one of the most famous Special Operations missions ever. Landing by helicopters flown by the Army's 160th Special Operations Aviation Regiment, the SEALs stormed inside bin Laden's compound and killed him.

Osama bin Laden's hideout in Abbottabad, Pakistan

SPECIAL OPERATIONS DOGS

On the mission to hunt down Osama bin Laden was a specially trained dog named Cairo. He was a Belgian Malinois, a breed that looks similar to the German shepherd but is slightly smaller. The Malinois is known for its strength and intelligence. After 9/11 the military began training dogs to go on special operations missions. The dogs can sniff out bombs as well as attack enemies. The dogs wear bulletproof vests and special gear that lets them **rappel** out of helicopters, just like people do. They can also parachute out of planes, sometimes attached to their human handler. It costs about $50,000 to train and deploy each special operations dog.

rappel—to lower oneself down with a rope

A Marine special ops group practices boarding and searching ships.

LOOKING AHEAD

Entering the 2010s the United States and its allies faced threats from new terrorist groups. U.S. special operations forces have the military skills to carry out attacks on these enemies. Some special operations troops speak the languages of the people the terrorists recruit. The Americans go into villages and gather intelligence. They can also win the trust of the local people, so they will help the United States and not the terrorists. They can also go behind enemy lines and rescue people held hostage by the terrorists.

Some military planners see special operations forces working more closely with regular troops. In the Army, for example, Green Berets and Rangers can provide information the other troops need. The regular troops can provide military support during Special Operations missions.

WOMEN LEADING THE WAY

To become a Ranger, Army troops have to complete Ranger School. Over two months they face a number of tough challenges, such as carrying heavy loads over long distances and into mountains. They train for up to 20 hours a day. No women had ever completed the training until Kristen Griest and Shaye Haver did it in 2015. Their success did not mean they automatically joined the 75th Ranger Regiment. It has its own requirements for joining, but Griest and Haver proved that women have the skills to be part of Special Operations. At the end of 2015, the U.S. Department of Defense announced a change in policy. It would let women join front-line combat troops, and those who qualify can try out for all of the military's Special Operations units.

On future missions, the Special Operations branches will get the best high-tech equipment available. For example, the Navy has been testing faster small boats that can carry SEALs on their secret missions.

No matter which military branch they serve in, U.S. Special Operations forces have proven to be among the world's best-trained and bravest troops. They play a key role in defending the United States.

SPECIAL OPERATIONS FORCES (2014)
Branch: Number of Personnel (approximate)

MARINES:
3,000

AIR FORCE:
18,000

ARMY:
29,000

NAVY:
8,800

GLOSSARY

airwing (AYR-wing)—a group of military aircraft

ally (AL-eye)—a person or country united with another for a common purpose

ambush (AM-bush)—a surprise attack

casualty (KAZH-oo-uhl-tee)—someone who is killed, wounded, or missing in a battle or in a war

civilian (si-VIL-yuhn)—a person who is not in the military

commando (kuh-MAN-doh)—specially trained soldier who can carry out surprise attacks, often in small groups

company (KUHM-puh-nee)—a U.S. military group made up of three to five platoons of soldiers

deactivate (dee-AK-tuh-vayt)—to take out of military duty

hostage (HOSS-tij)—a person held against his or her will

intelligence (in-TEL-uh-jenss)—secret information about an enemy's plans or action

nuclear (NOO-klee-ur)—having to do with the energy created by splitting atoms; nuclear bombs use this energy to cause an explosion.

obstacle (OB-stuh-kuhl)—something that gets in the way or prevents someone from doing something

rappel (ruh-PEL)—to lower oneself down with a rope

reconnaissance (ree-KAH-nuh-suhnss)—a mission to gather information about an enemy

resistance (ri-ZISS-tuhnss)—the people of an invaded nation who work together to drive out the invaders, often in secret

sabotage (SAB-uh-tahzh)—damage or destruction of property that is done on purpose

shell (SHEL)—a metal container filled with gunpowder and fired from a large gun

silencer (SYE-luhn-sur)—an attachment for a gun that reduces noise when the gun is fired

terrorist (TER-ur-ist)—someone who uses violence and threats to frighten people